All the world collected

poems by

Lynne Sherbondy

Finishing Line Press
Georgetown, Kentucky

All the world collected

ACKNOWLEDGMENTS

Special thanks to Jo Peterson for introducing me to poetry and Joan Moran for introducing me to life.

Publisher: Leah Huete de Maines
Editor: Christen Kincaid
Cover Art: "First" by Montine Jordan
Author Photo: Montine Jordan
Cover Design: Elizabeth Maines McCleavy

Order online: www.finishinglinepress.com
also available on amazon.com

Author inquiries and mail orders:
Finishing Line Press
PO Box 1626
Georgetown, Kentucky 40324
USA

Contents

For my brother

The lost year

Before all the air left her lungs,
she roused me from the linty La-Z-Boy
I slumbered in beside her
and muttered in my ear, "Gone."

I grabbed the small bag of things that matter
and waited there with her as careful strangers
covered the body then rolled it away
down an empty hall.

Outside, somewhere,
someone shouted about Jesus on a subway,
someone vomited up sadness on a sidewalk,
and the sun sank. Taking everything with it.

I pray a lot now

trying to reach the hotline in heaven
through a bruised and broken sky.
I don't get through, so I pray to you

in our old apartment off Central Park West,
with its useless a/c, kitchen the size of a sock,
and huge, drape-less windows for a view to a world

that wasn't ours. I try to recapture that
coconut whiskey smell of your Chanel 21,
but it's lost to the decades. Like you.

I pour a second cup of memory, take a sip,
and return to where we were
before everything went wrong:

Eyeing each other in that parking lot in Vegas
on that heat-beaten day in '78;
me fantasizing under the colorless sun

about what we might become together.
I wish today was yesterday
so we could still have tomorrow.

But it's not. I'm here, in an empty bed
in this lonely room, sending you another prayer.
Awaiting your reply.

It's 3AM

when the tie line to normalcy slackens
and lack of sleep gnaws away at me.

My eyes blink but won't stay shut.
I'm awake with worry and stare at the ceiling.
I know I should get up, turn on the light.

Instead, I sit in a wreckage of grief
in a dark patch of time's rough current,
where there's nothing to hold on to
as I watch the clock.

Sometimes at night

dread crawls into a corner
and sits with the people
who drift through my dreams.

My mother crouches there with them.

Tethered to a broken lifeline,
hair unwashed for weeks,
she smiles and says, "Don't worry.
There's a bigger plan."

Really?

Then surprise me with how time doesn't end
in a weedy tangle of misheard words,
a wasteland of what was.

The kindest ghost,
she always tries to calm me,
reminding me that,
"We're just passengers."

I've lost the comforter; I'm covered in sweat.
I wake up shaking and plead with her
not to leave.

My ragged mother clutches my hand,
sighs and closes her eyes.
Tells me to do the same.
"It's all just birth in reverse," she whispers.

A fast lightshow then back to God.

Five more minutes won't matter

when she slips into the black water
that fills the endless tunnel of time.

Sitting in the kitchen

it says here that some art speaks to us
and some wants us to tell it what it is.
I'm too tired to care.

My mother lies taut with exhaustion in the next room.
Each day, I go to her and we fight off the furies,
weep for what's gone before it leaves.

In the distance, I hear traffic, a hoot owl,
and some crazed squirrel playing with a ping pong ball
on an upturned stone. This is home in the country.

A soulless wind now swipes at the house
and another flurry of memories feather dusts around us
as I kneel at her bedside and lose her in the blizzard.

I dreamt I couldn't fall asleep

and woke exhausted.

In a foreign room, a sliver of light had flitted across a dirty floor
then found your bare feet as you slowly caressed my face.
I gagged on the sour fumes of our long-dead past.

I've tried to escape, but cannot leave.

So, please, Sleep, take me.

Upside down in the dentist's chair

The past floats back—minty—
as the sedative unspools the pain.

My tongue falls asleep first.

Then my parents wave at me from inside the mouth
of a yawning garage. Their clothes are the same color
as their bland stucco house. My mother tells me to
drive slowly, call when I get there. My father says
enjoy the ride, don't call for money. Or help.

He closes the door and I'm looking out a window

watching geese fly south the morning after 9/11.
A shard of sunlight hits the tip of a distant pine.
One lonely bluebird sees me, folded in my blanket
of bones, and starts to sing.

Suddenly on 59th Street, fingering decades of storefronts,

I enter Nirvana's revolving door to celebrate my 33rd birthday.
You're there ordering Indian food. You tell me to get as much
naan as I want and give me an expensive watch. We kiss and
feed each other random words that barely hint at who we are
or how long we'll last.

I turn away and find myself hiding in a fortress of brittle twigs and
branches.

My little brother is with me. We huddle together
as howling marauders pelt our makeshift fort
with rocks and crayons. He starts to cry.
I put him on my back and tell him we're going to make a run for it

when consciousness chews through and reclaims the light.

The dentist says he's done.
I wobble toward the open door.
It's not an easy exit.

Goodbye, my golden city

and your filthy, rutted rails,
dark and wet with garbage
and lost clothing, where ten-inch rats
dine and hungry musicians play
on the platform.

Goodbye, slow trundle up Columbus
as winter dusk pinches the sky and
the red light atop the Empire Hotel
guides me home — young and drunk
from draining four bottles of cheap pinot
with two friends I think I'll have forever,
but won't.

Goodbye, aimless sex and five AM pit stops
at a 24-hour diner with famous onion soup
that steadies me for the cramped sidewalks,
crowded agendas, sullen eyes and empty stares,
all on my way to work.

Goodbye, Friday night haunt in Hell's Kitchen
with the disarming art on the bathroom walls
and cocoon-like booths that held us together
through blizzards, break-ups, lost jobs,
and let me walk away
with a buzz that dulled and blurred our differences.

Goodbye, my golden city.
Your hope is like snow.
Beautiful, but brief.
I left and not even your voice survives.
Now I have keys to a door that's not mine.
And I can't touch you.

Marking the days

Not quite drowned, I'm washed back to shore,
coughing up lies (again) on the wrong side of sick;
pretending it's fine, begging death to wake me.

There's a man alone in a boat

on a river that doesn't move.
Almost naked, but not nude,
he's not rowing, not fishing;
he just smokes and waits.

I wave to him; he doesn't wave back.
I'm alone, too, waiting for something
that doesn't move, or simply refuses
to arrive.

A line of geese

a loose stitch in the sky, heads north of the clear mirror lake,
then west of the wound on my wrist where the wreckage of my life
has begun.

I watch them and keep walking—past old pines that, like old men,
chase warmth but fear the wind. I fear what's chasing me and pull a
sleeve over my scar.

Fall is near. I feel it. The light changes. I search for the geese.
Smaller birds now surf a breeze above me. I'm getting cold.

The splintered voice buried in my chest tells me to think about my
family and keep walking even as bloodthirsty time follows me home.

Watching a girl plant a tree

in a fenced yard similar to the one where we played.
Oh, that yard and the fragile home we held onto.

We're well outside the fence now,
where nothing is safe and everything vanishes.
But hopefully not this tree.

I take its picture and watch the girl water its soil.
She drops the hose and walks away, not bothering to latch the gate.
"Go back! Go back and lock it. Keep it safe," I want to yell but don't.

I leave the windows rolled up and drive off.
She's too young to know how fast things change
or where life can go.

I came to enlightenment late

Driving home tonight,
under trees weighted with winter,
the city rushes over me—
that slab of humanity
that kneaded me into who I am now:
just a face in the mirror,
sad beyond sorrow,
a bubble away from bursting.

I read somewhere that God is everything that was
before nothing was, and all that will be
when everything is gone. Fair enough,
but where is he now as I tear up and turn the corner,
lumbering along beneath the day's deep shadows.

I've grown numb to the sound of you not here,
though I still hear your laugh
when you'd do that little dance you only did for me,
reluctantly, with your glasses on upside down.

As I make my way to the house,
a knot of moonlight finds the path.
Inside, I light a fire, listen to the hiss.
Behind me is the place where we'd sit for hours
with an Argentinian red and talk about our future
before it fell into this dark well.

But that was love, and this is life.
Furious, I feed the fire and sweep
the ash.

The night explodes

I'm ten years old, riding a Western Flyer
on a gray Thanksgiving Day
around empty suburban streets,

past small yards
where the Bermuda grass has turned
but the fruitless mulberries remain.

The air smells sweet and burnt
from pinon pine charcoaling down
in out-of-place fireplaces.

No one in our desert neighborhood needs
a fireplace, but everybody has one.
Except us.

I lift my hands into the air
and let the bike steer my escape.
I fly past the decades

of dinners with a drunk,
forced catechisms with unhappy nuns,
and rootless friendships found in a gambling town.

I never retake the handlebars.
I stop riding in circles
and let the circle break.

The world collected

Free delivery,
thin crust pizza,
jalapeno jelly,
Cosmopolitans,
laser surgery,
earmuffs,
stretch jeans,
snowblowers,
handwarmers,
instant ice packs,
timed sprinklers,
dryer balls,
terrycloth robes,
tomato cages,
Mr. Coffee,
aromatherapy,
psychotherapy,
immunotherapy—

none of it kept time from taking her face.
Yet life put its fingers on us
and bent us with hope.

There was heartbreak, but also happiness
as beautiful as a butterfly kiss,
as welcome as curbside pickup.

Lynne Sherbondy grew up in Las Vegas amidst mobsters, showgirls, and nuclear testing. But that's for another bio.

She began writing poetry in her teens, won a few contests, and got published in two anthologies. She planned to become a poet—but film, theater, and television beckoned. Lynne moved to NYC and worked for years writing and producing award-winning videos. During this time, several of her plays and screenplays garnered interest from both theatrical and film producers. She also served as a Story Analyst for Academy Award-winning film director, Jonathan Demme, and Story Editor for Vanguard Films, where she created and developed an incredibly ill-fated sitcom. Lately, her creative life has come full circle. The poetry she put on a back burner has now reclaimed center stage.

Lynne holds a BA in Theatre Arts from the University of Nevada, Las Vegas; a MS in Counseling from Fordham University; and an MFA in Film from Columbia University. She lives in upstate New York with her partner and two chihuahuas.